T0070991

Bob Chilcott

Mo Li Hua 茉莉花

5 ARRANGEMENTS OF CHINESE SONGS

MUSIC DEPARTMENT

OXFORD
UNIVERSITY PRESS

OXFORD
UNIVERSITY PRESS

Great Clarendon Street, Oxford OX2 6DP,
United Kingdom

Oxford University Press is a department of the University of Oxford.
It furthers the University's objective of excellence in research, scholarship,
and education by publishing worldwide. Oxford is a registered trade mark of
Oxford University Press in the UK and in certain other countries

© Oxford University Press 2015

Bob Chilcott has asserted his right under the Copyright, Designs
and Patents Act, 1988, to be identified as the Arranger of these Works

Database right Oxford University Press (maker)

First published 2015

Impression: 1

All rights reserved. No part of this publication may be reproduced,
stored in a retrieval system, or transmitted, in any form or by any means,
without the prior permission in writing of Oxford University Press

Permission to perform the works in this anthology in public
(except in the course of divine worship) should normally be obtained
from the Performing Right Society Ltd (PRS) at www.prsformusic.com
or a local performing right licensing organization, unless the owner or the
occupier of the premises being used already holds a licence from such an
organization. Likewise, permission to make and exploit a recording must
be obtained in advance from the Mechanical-Copyright Protection
Society Ltd (MCPS) at www.prsformusic.com or from a local mechanical
copyright licensing organization

Enquiries concerning reproduction outside the scope of the above should be
directed to the Music Rights Department, Oxford University Press, at
music.permissions.uk@oup.com or at the address above

ISBN 978-0-19-340421-2

Music and text origination by
Andrew Jones
Printed in Great Britain on acid-free paper by
Halstan & Co. Ltd, Amersham, Bucks.

Contents

Composer's Note / 作曲家寄语 4

My Flower / 我的花儿 / 我的花兒 5

Shepherd's Song / 牧歌 13

Sun is Out / 太阳出来喜洋洋 / 太陽出來喜洋洋 17

In Sichuan / 下四川 22

Mo Li Hua (Jasmine Flower) / 茉莉花 32

Composer's Note

I was asked by David Hill and the Bach Choir to arrange a Chinese folk song for their tour of China in 2014, and I prepared a version of the lovely song 'Mo li Hua'. I loved the melody, which spins its fragile line and, in a Western sense, ends unresolved. With the help of Francesca Mosely, I identified a few more songs from different areas of the country: songs that tell of the beauty of nature, the simplicity of life, and, of course, love. 'Shepherd's Song' was suggested to me by Lin Chun-lung, and I dedicate the remaining four songs in the collection to him and his choir, the Shanghai TMC Mixed Chamber Choir (operated by the Taipei Male Choir). I am grateful both to Francesca and Chun-lung for giving me a glimpse of the diverse and rich culture expressed through each of these songs. They are, of course, arranged from a very Western perspective, but I hope that all types of singers will enjoy the beauty and energy of these traditional melodies. I am also grateful to Sean Bui for his considered editorial work on this publication.

Bob Chilcott

作曲家寄语

二〇一四年，大卫•希尔 (David Hill) 及英国巴赫合唱团 (The Bach Choir) 邀请我为其在华演出之旅改编一首中国民歌，我便准备了著名中国民歌《茉莉花》。我非常喜爱《茉莉花》，优美动听的旋律勾勒出花朵娇弱的线条，曲终余音绕梁，让人意犹未尽。在莫鸣 (Francesca Mosely) 的帮助下，我找到了另外几首中国民歌，歌曲诉说自然之美、生活之简、当然，还有爱情之甜。林俊龙向我推荐了内蒙民歌《牧歌》，我也将本曲集后期改编之四首歌献给他及其合唱团——上海拉纤人室内混声合唱团（由台北拉纤人男声合唱团运营）。非常感谢莫鸣和林俊龙，让我透过这些民歌得以一瞥丰富多彩的中华文化。虽然五首民歌以西方人的视角进行改编，但我希望各类型的歌手都能享受这传统旋律传达的美好与活力。最后也要感谢尚恩•裴对本谱集的悉心编辑。

鲍勃•契尔考特

作曲家寄语

二〇一四年，大衛•希爾 (David Hill) 及英國巴赫合唱團 (The Bach Choir) 邀請我為其在華演出之旅改編一首中國民歌，我便準備了著名中國民歌《茉莉花》。我非常喜愛《茉莉花》，優美動聽的旋律勾勒出花朵嬌弱的線條，曲終餘音繞樑，讓人意猶未盡。在莫鳴 (Francesca Mosely) 的幫助下，我找到了另外幾首中國民歌，歌曲訴說自然之美、生活之簡、當然，還有愛情之甜。林俊龍向我推薦了內蒙民歌《牧歌》，我也將本曲集後期改編之四首歌獻給他及其合唱團——上海拉縴人室內混聲合唱團（由台北拉縴人男聲合唱團運營）。非常感謝莫鳴和林俊龍，讓我透過這些民歌得以一瞥豐富多彩的中華文化。雖然五首民歌以西方人的視角進行改編，但我希望各類型的歌手都能享受這傳統旋律傳達的美好與活力。最後也要感謝尚恩•裴對本譜集的悉心編輯。

鮑勃•契爾考特

for Lin Chun-Lung and the Shanghai TMC Mixed Chamber Choir

My Flower
我的花儿 /我的花兒

English words by Bob Chilcott

Trad. Chinese
arr. BOB CHILCOTT (b. 1955)

© Oxford University Press 2015. Photocopying this copyright material is ILLEGAL.

12
心 花 开 放, 美 丽 的 姑 娘 我 的 花
danc-ing with the flow'rs; Beau-ti-ful girl, my flow'r, you bring me
心 花 開 放, 美 麗 的 姑 娘 我 的 花
16
儿, 我 要 欢 笑 欢 笑, 哎 呀 呀!
joy, you bring me hap-pi-ness; ah ya ya ya!
兒, 我 要 歡 笑 歡 笑, 哎 呀 呀!
22
S.
A.
ah
mf
2. 你 好 比 是 那 海
2. You are as the sea, my be-
2. 你 好 比 是 那 海
mf
T.
B.

28
mf
ah
洋, 哎 我 是 那 海 鸥 永 远 在
-lov - - ed, I an o - cean bird, fly - ing a-
洋, 哎 我 是 那 海 鷗 永 遠 在
33
海 面 飞 翔, 美 丽 的 姑 娘 我 的 花 儿, 我 要 欢
- bove you in the sky; Beau-ti-ful girl, my flow'r, you bring me joy, you bring me
海 麵 飛 翔, 美 麗 的 姑 娘 我 的 花 兒, 我 要 歡

38
ah
笑 欢 笑, 哎 呀 呀!
hap - pi - ness; ah ya ya ya!
笑 歡 笑, 哎 呀 呀!
ah
43
mf
3. 你 的 名 字 多 香
3. You are sweet and fair, my be -
3. 你 的 名 字 多 香
mf

49
f
甜, 哎 苗 条 的 姑 娘 我 把
-lov - - ed, All that I wish for you is the
甜, 哎 苗 條 的 姑 娘 我 把
f
f
54
酥 油 献 给 你, 美 丽 的 姑 娘 我 的 花
fi - nest I can give; Beau - ti - ful girl, my flow'r, you bring me
酥 油 獻 給 你, 美 麗 的 姑 娘 我 的 花

58
儿，我要欢 笑 欢 笑，哎呀 呀！
joy, you bring me hap - pi - ness; ah ya ya ya!
兒，我要歡 笑 歡 笑，哎呀 呀！
63
ff

68
ff
4. 虽 然 我 们 刚 相 见, 哎
4. Though we're new - ly met, my be - lov - - ed,
4. 雖 然 我 們 剛 相 見, 哎
ff
73
多 情 的 眼 睛, 我 一 见 你 就 倾 心,
When I see your eyes, my heart is danc - ing with the flow'rs;
多 情 的 眼 睛, 我 一 見 你 就 傾 心,

77
美 丽 的 姑 娘 我 的 花 儿, 我 要 欢 笑 欢
Beau - ti - ful girl, my flow'r, you bring me joy, you bring me hap - pi - ness;
美 麗 的 姑 娘 我 的 花 兒, 我 要 歡 笑 歡
81
1.
2.
poco rit.
fff
笑, 哎 呀 呀! 笑, 哎 呀 呀!
ah ya ya ya! ah ya ya ya!
笑, 哎 呀 呀! 笑, 哎 呀 呀!
fff
1.
2.
poco rit.
fff

for Lin Chun-Lung and the Shanghai TMC Mixed Chamber Choir

Shepherd's Song
牧歌

English words by Bob Chilcott

Eastern Mongolian Folksong
arr. BOB CHILCOTT (b. 1955)

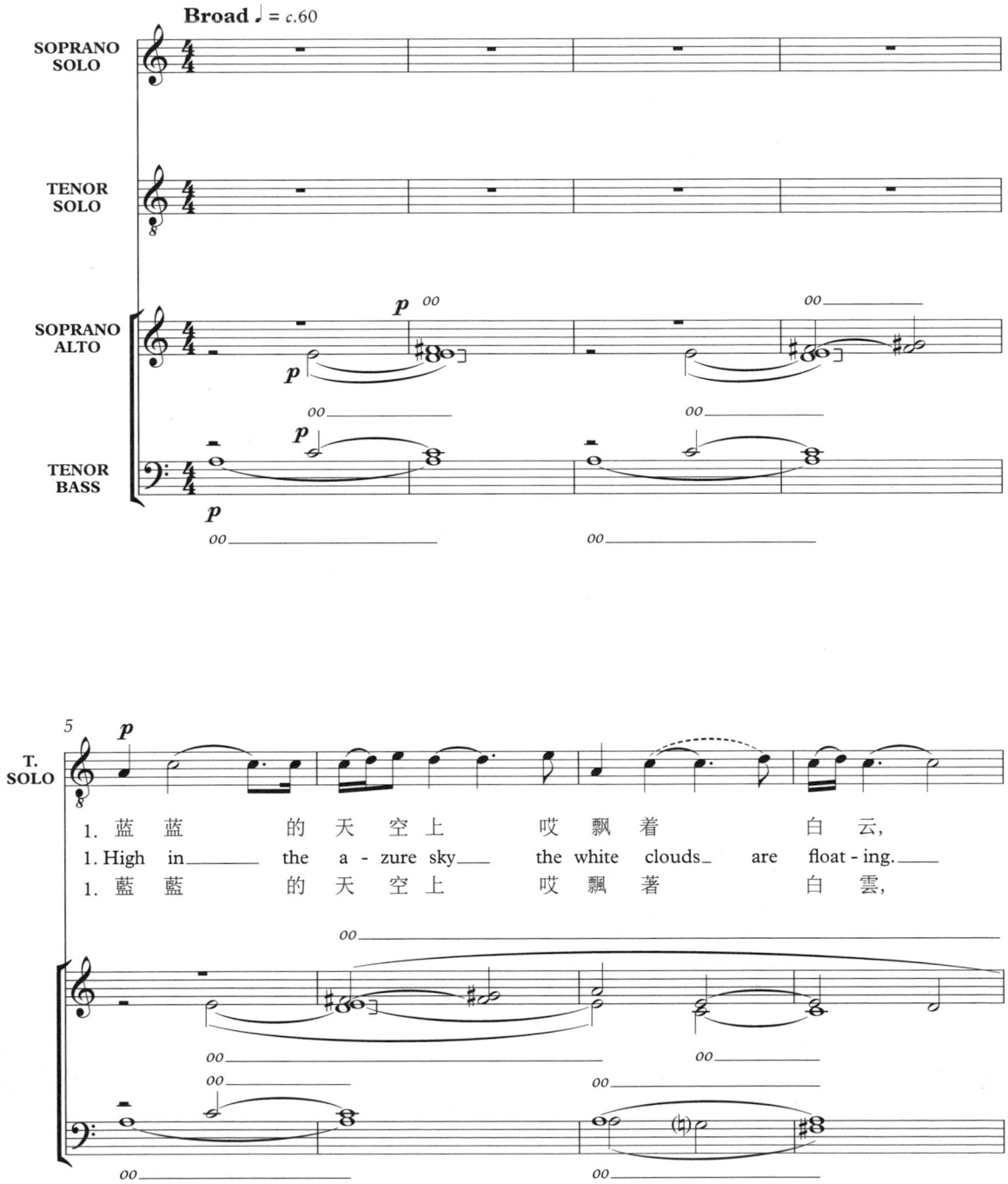

© Oxford University Press 2015. Photocopying this copyright material is ILLEGAL.

9
T. SOLO
白 云 的 下 面 跑 着 雪 白 的 羊 群。
Young flocks be-neath them show their lus-tre, as white as gold.
白 雲 的 下 麵 跑 著 雪 白 的 羊 群。
S. A.
T. B.
oo
13
羊 群 好 像 是 斑 斑 的 白 银,
Bright gold-en light re-flects on the mea-dow,
羊 群 好 像 是 斑 斑 的 白 銀,
mf
18
mp
2. 羊 群 好 像 是 斑 斑 的 白 银,
2. Bright, bright gold-en light re-flects on the mea-dow,
2. 羊 群 好 像 是 斑 斑 的 白 銀,
mp 羊 群
Bright
羊 群

洒 在 草 原 上 多 么 爱 煞 人 呦
Paint - ing a pic - ture of joy un - told.
灑 在 草 原 上 多 么 爱 煞 人 呦
22
mp
草 原 上 爱 煞 人 呦 爱 煞
Paint - ing a pic- ture of joy, joy un-
草 原 上 爱 煞 人 呦 爱 煞
mp
草 原 上 爱 煞 人 呦 爱 煞
Paint - ing a pic - ture of joy, joy un-
草 原 上 爱 煞 人 呦 爱 煞
26
p
oo
oo
人 呦。
-told. oo oo oo
人 呦。
p
人 呦。
-told. oo oo oo
人 呦。
31
S. SOLO
p
ah
T. SOLO
p
3. 翠 绿 的 草 地 上 哎 跑 着 白 羊,
3. Green fields a - round us with white flock a - bound-ing,
3. 翠 綠 的 草 地 上 哎 跑 著 白 羊,
oo
S. A.
oo
oo
oo
oo
T. B.
oo
oo

35
ah
羊 群 像 珍 珠 洒 在 绿 绒 上。
Show - ing their beau-ty, their beau - ty in the sun.
羊 群 像 珍 珠 灑 在 綠 絨 上。
39
rit.
pp
pp

Sun is Out
太阳出来喜洋洋 / 太陽出來喜洋洋

English words by Bob Chilcott

Trad. Chinese
arr. BOB CHILCOTT (b. 1955)

© Oxford University Press 2015. Photocopying this copyright material is ILLEGAL.

12
上 山 崗 欧 啰 啰!
Off we go, ah ya ya!
上 山 崗 歐 啰 啰!
17
f
T.
B.
2. 手 里 拿 把 啰 儿! 开 山 斧 欧 郎 啰!
2. At the rea - dy, ah ya! Axe in hand, ah ya ya!
2. 手 裏 拿 把 啰 兒! 開 山 斧 歐 郎 啰!
21
不 怕 虎 豹 郎 郎 扯 光 扯! 和 豺 狼 欧 啰
Ti - gers, jack - als, ah ya ya ya ya! We don't care, ah ya
不 怕 虎 豹 郎 郎 扯 光 扯! 和 豺 狼 歐 啰

25
S.
A.
3. 悬 岩 陡 坎 啰 儿!
3. Rocks and ridg-es, ah ya!
3. 懸 岩 陡 坎 啰 兒!
T.
B.
啰!
ya!
啰!
31
不 稀 罕 欧 郎 啰! 唱 起 歌 儿 郎 郎 扯 光 扯!
Show no fear, ah ya ya! Gath'-ring fire-wood, ah ya ya ya ya!
不 稀 罕 歐 郎 啰! 唱 起 歌 兒 郎 郎 扯 光 扯!

36
忙 砍 柴 欧 啰 啰!
We all sing, ah ya ya!
忙 砍 柴 歐 啰 啰!

41
4. 走 了 一 山 啰 儿! 又 一 山 欧 郎 啰!
4. Cross the moun-tain, ah ya! Then one more, ah ya ya!
4. 走 了 一 山 啰 兒! 又 一 山 歐 郎 啰!
4. 走 了 一 山 啰 儿! 又 一 山 欧 郎 啰! 这 山 去 了
4. Cross the moun-tain, ah ya! Then one more, ah ya ya! Then a-no-ther,
4. 走 了 一 山 啰 兒! 又 一 山 歐 郎 啰! 這 山 去 了

46
ff
这 山 去 了 郎 郎 扯 光 扯! 那 山 来 欧 啰
Then a - no - ther, ah ya ya ya ya! One more gone, ah ya
這 山 去 了 郎 郎 扯 光 扯! 那 山 來 歐 啰
ff
郎 郎 扯 光 扯! 那 山 来 欧 啰 啰!
ah ya ya ya ya! One more gone, ah ya ya!
郎 郎 扯 光 扯! 那 山 來 歐 啰 啰!
ff
50
啰!
ya!
啰!
5. 只 要 我 们 啰 儿!
5. Food and cloth - ing, ah ya!
5. 衹 要 我 們 啰 兒!

55
多 勤 快 欧 郎 啰! 不 愁 吃 来 郎 郎 扯 光 扯!
We don't care, ah ya ya! Work - ing, liv - ing, ah ya ya ya ya!
多 勤 快 歐 郎 啰! 不 愁 吃 來 郎 郎 扯 光 扯!
60
不 愁 穿 欧 啰 啰!
Sun is out, ah ya ya!
不 愁 穿 歐 啰 啰!

for Lin Chun-Lung and the Shanghai TMC Mixed Chamber Choir

In Sichuan
下四川

English words by Bob Chilcott

Trad. Chinese
arr. BOB CHILCOTT (b. 1955)

© Oxford University Press 2015. Photocopying this copyright material is ILLEGAL.

11
mp cresc.
f
哟, 噢 两 噢, 噢
oh, o - ver the moun - tain, o - ver the
哟, 噢 兩 噢, 噢
mp cresc.
f
mp cresc.
f
16
dim.
mp
溜 溜 儿 山, 三 溜 溜 山 哎 脚 户 歌
moun-tain - side, On and on, my swift - foot-ed
溜 溜 兒 山, 三 溜 溜 山 哎 腳 戶 歌
dim.
mp
dim.
mp

21
mf
下 了 这 四 川, 噢 哟
lov - er's in Si - chuan, Oh, oh,
下 了 這 四 川, 噢 哟
mf
mf
25
dim.
哟 啊 脚 户 歌 下 了 这 四
oh, my swift - foot - ed lov - er's in Si -
哟 啊 腳 戶 歌 下 了 這 四
dim.
dim.

29
p
川。
-chuan.
川。
p
p
34
p cresc.
2. 今 个 子 牵 来 者
2. Lead - ing me on - ward,
2. 今 個 子 牽 來 者
p cresc.
cresc.

39
mp cresc.
f
哟, 噢 明 噢 噢
oh, lead-ing me on - ward till to -
哟, 噢 明 噢 噢
mp cresc.
f
mp cresc.
f
44
dim.
mp
个 子 牵, 每 日 牵 啊 夜 夜 的
-mor - row comes, On and on, in the hope I
個 子 牽, 每 日 牽 啊 夜 夜 的
dim.
mp
dim.
mp

49
mf
晚 夕 里 梦 见, 噢, 哟
meet you in my dreams, Oh, oh
晚 夕 裏 夢 見, 噢, 哟
mf
mf
53
dim.
哟, 啊 夜 夜 的 晚 夕 里 梦
oh, in the hope I meet you in my
哟, 啊 夜 夜 的 晚 夕 裏 夢
dim.
dim.

57
p
见。
dreams.
見。
p
p
62
p cresc.
3. 脚 踏 上 大 路
3. Step - ping on - ward,
3. 腳 踏 上 大 路
p cresc.
cresc.

67
mp cresc.
f
哟, 噢 心 噢 噢
oh, step - ping on - ward, with
哟, 噢 心 噢 噢
mp cresc.
f
mp cresc.
f
72
dim.
mp
想 着 你, 心 想 着 你 啊 喝 油 也
you in my heart, On and on, I long for the
想 著 你, 心 想 著 你 啊 喝 油 也
dim.
mp
dim.
mp

77
mf
不 着 肉 了, 噢 哟
mo - ment you come back to me, Oh, oh,
不 著 肉 了, 噢 哟
mf
mf
81
dim.
哟 啊 喝 油 也 不 着 肉
oh, I long for the mo - ment you come back to
哟 啊 喝 油 也 不 著 肉
dim.
dim.

85
p
me.
p
p
89
rit.
rit.

for David Hill and The Bach Choir

Mo Li Hua
(Jasmine Flower)
茉莉花

English words by Bob Chilcott

Trad. Chinese
arr. BOB CHILCOTT (b. 1955)

© Oxford University Press 2015. Photocopying this copyright material is ILLEGAL.

9
满 园 花 开 香 也 香 不 过 它,
Your sweet - est fra - grance lin - gers, lin - gers in the air;
滿 園 花 開 香 也 香 不 過 它,
13
我 有 心 采 一 朵 戴 又 怕 看 花 的
If I were to pluck your blos - som, Ev' - ry - one would scold me for
我 有 心 採 一 朵 戴 又 怕 看 花 的
17
S.
人 儿 骂。
what I had done.
人 兒 罵。
mp
2. 好 一 朵
2. Oh, my
2. 好 一 朵
T.
mp
2. 好 一 朵 茉 莉
2. Oh, my jas - mine
2. 好 一 朵 茉 莉
mp

21
mf
茉 莉 花, 好 一 朵 茉 莉 花, 茉 莉
jas - mine flow'r, Oh, my jas - mine flow'r; Your fin-
茉 莉 花, 好 一 朵 茉 莉 花, 茉 莉
mf
花, 好 一 朵 茉 莉 花, 茉 莉
flow'r, Oh, my jas - mine flow'r; Your fin - est
花, 好 一 朵 茉 莉 花, 茉 莉
mf
25
mp
花 开 雪 也 白 不过它, 我 有
- est bloom is whit - er, whit - er than the snow; If I
花 開 雪 也 白 不過它, 我 有
mp
花 开 雪 也 白 不过 它, 我 有 心
bloom is whit-er, whit - er than the snow; If I were to
花 開 雪 也 白 不過 它, 我 有 心
mp

29
心 采 一 朵 戴 又 怕 旁 人 笑
were to pluck your blos - som, Ev' - ry - one would mock me for what
心 採 一 朵 戴 又 怕 旁 人 笑
采 一 朵 戴 又 怕 旁 人 笑
pluck your blos-som, Ev' - ry - one would mock me for what I had
採 一 朵 戴 又 怕 旁 人 笑
33
p
话。
I had done.
話。
p
话。
done.
話。
p

38
p dolce
S.
A.
3. 好 一 朵 茉 莉 花, 好 一 朵 茉 莉
3. Oh, my jas - mine flow'r, Oh, my jas - mine
3. 好 一 朵 茉 莉 花, 好 一 朵 茉 莉
T.
B.
p dolce
满 园
Your beau - ty
滿 園
42
花, 满 园 花 开 比 也 比 一 不 过
flow'r; Your beau - ty all sur - pass - ing, all sur - pass - ing
花, 滿 園 花 開 比 也 比 一 不 過

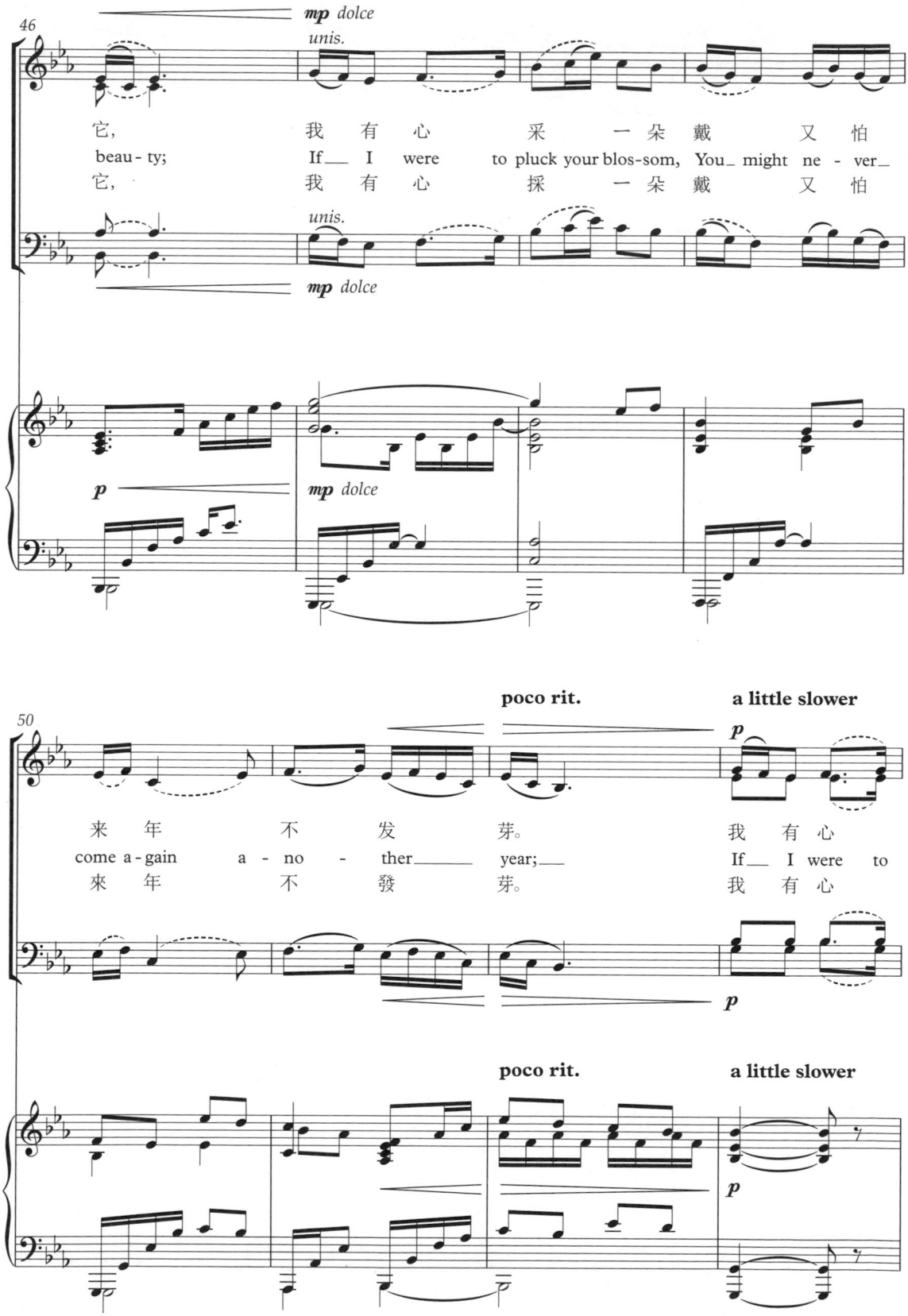
46
mp dolce
unis.
它, 我 有 心 采 一 朵 戴 又 怕
beau - ty; If I were to pluck your blos-som, You might ne - ver
它, 我 有 心 採 一 朵 戴 又 怕
unis.
mp dolce
p
mp dolce
50
poco rit.
a little slower
p
来 年 不 发 芽。 我 有 心
come a - gain a - no - ther year; If I were to
來 年 不 發 芽。 我 有 心
p
poco rit.
a little slower
p

poco rit.
54
采 一 朵 戴 又 怕 来 年 不 发
pluck your blos-som You_ might ne - ver_ come a-gain a - no - ther_____
採 一 朵 戴 又 怕 來 年 不 發
poco rit.
a tempo
rit.
pp
58
芽。
year._____
芽。
pp
a tempo
rit.
pp